P9-DTO-901

Claudia Strand

LOOK AT ME!

THE ART OF THE PORTRAIT

PRESTEL

Munich • London • New York

Table of Contents

Follow these clues!

Albrecht Dürer,
Self-portrait,
1484,
Albertina,
Vienna

Turn On the Spotlight!

Do you sometimes have the feeling that you're being watched? You're walking along the street and **suddenly someone's looking at you**. Only on second glance do you realize that **it's just a picture**.

Pictures of people are with us throughout our lives. **Faces** look out at us from the pages of newspapers and magazines and look down from **advertising posters and billboards**. We see them in motion on TV, in movies, and on the internet. You might know some of them, even their **names**, in which case you already know more about them than their appearance alone tells you.

Can you remember the first picture of a person you ever made? Surely not. It was most likely some strange creature with a round body, to which thin arms and legs were attached. At the time, you may have known very well who it was meant to be. But you probably would no longer have any idea if you saw it again. Of course, your drawing abilities have likely improved since then. Instead of making "stick figures," you may be able to draw pictures with real people in them, so that everyone can tell who they're supposed to be.

When you look through your family's collection of photos, you'll also find many **pictures from your life.** Perhaps they bring back memories of a vacation, or you see yourself in a photo of your **first day at school.** Maybe you'll find pictures in which you were so small, you can't even remember the places and things they show anymore.

It's truly remarkable how pictures **can bring back times that are long gone**. And of course, that's exactly what they've always been meant to do. Each century has had its own ideas about how to represent people … and its own **tricks** for doing so. This is why pictures tell stories about the people they show. **They describe those people's lives and the times in which they lived.** So every picture you look at is also a **journey through time,** one that sometimes goes back very, very far into the past.

In art, a picture of a person is called a portrait.
A portrait represents a person and "casts light" on something, like when a photographer aims a **spotlight** at a model during a photo shoot. A portrait also tries to show what kind of person the sitter is and how he or she feels: **happy, sad, withdrawn, open, secretive, stern …**

Painters, sculptors, and photographers need a lot of time and patience to make images like this. And you, the viewer, also need time and patience to fully understand a well-made portrait. Sometimes you need to **pretend you're a detective and pay close attention to all the clues**. Is the person looking straight out at you or to the side? Is he or she shown in full-length or only in part? Does the person have specific features or attributes that tell you something about his or her life? **Anything** can provide an important clue!

This is why deciphering portraits is not always so easy. The older they are, the more complicated they can be. Some portraits simply don't want to divulge their secrets all at once.

Photo in the Louvre, **People looking at the** Mona Lisa, 2005

The World's Most Famous Portrait

There's one portrait that you probably know. It has kept its secret for over 500 years, and it is **very closely guarded.** Today, you can admire it only from a safe distance **behind bullet-proof glass.** Do you already know what portrait it is? If you guessed the Mona Lisa, you're right. Believe it or not, the Mona Lisa was actually **stolen** once - and then returned. Another time, it was damaged when someone threw a stone at it!

Portraits can be loved or hated, protected or destroyed. They can seem almost as "alive" as real people, even though they may not depict their subjects very accurately. In the case of the **Mona Lisa,** we still aren't entirely sure whom the artist, **Leonardo da Vinci,** was actually painting. **Was it really the wife of Count Francesco del Giocondo, as many believe? And why is she smiling so mysteriously?** Many scholars have tried to find out.

Learning how to understand and decipher portraits requires the **skill of a detective** and **a love of discovery.** To make portraits yourself, you'll need **a tiny bit of courage,** because portraits can always reveal new and unsuspected things: both about others and about you. Sometimes you can even uncover little secrets.

This is Mona Lisa

This is me

Attach a photo of
yourself here.

Leonardo da Vinci, **Mona Lisa,**
1503-1507, Louvre, Paris

Your name

This is what you look like today. Anyone would be able to recognize you right away in this photo. But maybe you're planning to cut your hair short or let it grow long? Or maybe you'll get a new pair of glasses? Your appearance will surely change over time in many ways.

But despite this, you will always stay who you are.
You have your own way of expressing yourself, which
will always remain unmistakably yours.

Now let's try another way to make a basic self-portrait. Answer the following questions about yourself, including your eye color, height, and birthday.

This is Me

This questionnaire will be easy for you to complete. If there's anything you're not sure about, just look in the mirror ...

First name/ middle name: ....

Last name: ....

Date of birth: ....

Citizenship: ....

Signature: ....

My face is:
O oval
O round
□ angular

My nose is:
□ long
□ short
O broad
□ thin
O round
□ pointy

My eyes are:
O blue
O green
O brown
O another color ....
□ large
□ small
O round
o almond-shaped
□ a different shape

My hair is:
□ long
□ short
□ straight
O wavy
O curly
O blond
□ brown
□ black
O red
O another color
O my favorite hairstyle ....

Special distinguishing features:
O glasses
O braces
O other ....

Height ....
Shoe size ....

My favorite color ....
My favorite animal ....

You can experiment with your own portrait just as artists **throughout history** have always done. Maybe you'll discover something about yourself along the way …

Have you always wondered what you might look like with red hair?
Would you like to seem wild and dangerous or as delicate as an elf?
Maybe you'd prefer cool sunglasses?
You can also try to hide by slipping behind a "mask."

Read how on page 85.

The cool guy with the sunglasses in the picture to the right is a famous French poet, Guillaume Apollinaire. He was painted by the Italian artist Giorgio de Chirico. But does the portrait truly reveal the personality of this man? He's as pale as a statue and his eyes are hidden behind his sunglasses. **Is he concealing something? It's also possible to hide in a portrait.**

Giorgio de Chirico,
Guillaume Apollinaire, 1914,
Centre Georges Pompidou, Pari

Eyes, Nose, Mouth – How to Paint a Portrait?

As we discovered earlier, **the very first drawings** you made of people - possibly of yourself or your family - **don't look very much like** the real human beings. But one thing about these pictures is obvious: **They are people.**

What has to be on a face - or rather in a face - to make it look like one? **Eyes, a nose, and a mouth,** of course. The **shape of the face** is also important. Is it thin or wide? Does it have a double chin or a pointed one?

Would you like to draw or paint a face? You could also cut a silhouette out of construction paper (find out how on page 19). There are **many possible ways** to make a portrait.

Dot, dot, comma, dash:
a smiling face in a flash.

If you know how to use a computer, you can create a face on the website http://www.ctapt.de/flashface.

At the end of the book, there's an illustration you can color or decorate however you'd like.

See how on page 85.

Tullio Pericoli is an Italian artist. In this picture, he has neatly attached a few eye-nose-mouth variations and hung some ears from the ear to the right. You can copy the picture; cut out the eyes, noses, and mouths; and then reassemble them as you wish. **But be careful:** not every eye or every mouth makes the same impression. Whether the eye is looking at you in a friendly way or is scowling angrily, or whether the mouth is smiling at you or yawning in boredom, they all merge together to form a **specific facial expression.** And here you can decide how to combine them.

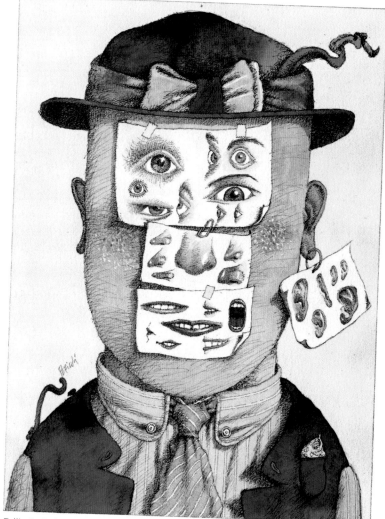

Tullio Pericoli, **Uncompleted Portrait,** 1985

Paul Klee, **The Black Prince,** 1927,
Kunstsammlung Nordrhein-Westfalen, Düsseldorf

Turn on the lights!
A Prince Looks out from the Darkness

Do you sometimes look out the window in the evening? Maybe you like to take a peek before you go to bed, or when you're tucked up in your soft blankets and pillows? Things that seem so familiar during the day can **take on a new life** at night. In the **darkened world** they suddenly seem alien, especially if they're illuminated by the moon or by a streetlight.

Glowing Faces

When a face emerges out of the darkness, it can look unreal. Sometimes you're startled, even though you may know the person well. When light falls on a face, its expression changes or begins **to glow as if from within**. German artist Paul Klee captured this effect in his picture, **The Black Prince.** Klee's figure seems a bit **unworldly**, looking out of the painting with green eyes like a panther: a gaze from a strange and distant land.

Draw a simple face like the prince's on a sheet of black cardboard or poster board and cut out the features. Then, on the back, glue colored transparent paper or tissue paper over the openings. When you light a small candle and place it behind the black cardboard, the face will literally glow.

Look to the left, look to the right, just look away

There are many kinds of portraits.
Some show the **whole person,** the entire figure. You can see one of these on page 49 of this book. It's a famous self-portrait of an artist! But others show only the face, the place where a person's feelings are expressed most clearly.

A view of the face seen directly from the front is called a **full-face or frontal view.**

A view from the side is called a **profile,**

while a **three-quarter profile** shows part of the other side of the face.

If the upper body is also shown, this is called **a bust portrait or half-length portrait.**

Silhouettes

There's a romantic story about the origin of
the **silhouette**:

A long time ago, in ancient Greece, there lived a potter
named Butades of Sicyon. His daughter was filled with
sorrow, for she could not bear to leave her lover. But
a great idea sprang up from her grief. In order to have
her beloved with her always, she copied his shadow
onto the wall. Her father formed the outline with clay
and fired the likeness in the kiln. Thus, a silhouette of his
face was made from light and shadow. In this way, the
very first such portrait was formed out of love.

Goethe und Fritz von Stein.

Silhouettes were **all the rage** in the eighteenth century. This is when the famous German poet, Johann Wolfgang von Goethe, lived. Goethe was also very talented at drawing, as you can see in this silhouette, where he depicted himself together with a young friend.

Johann Wolfgang von Goethe,
**Johann Wolfgang von Goethe
and Gottlob Friedrich Constantin
Freiherr von Stein of Kochberg,**
ca. 1783, Goethe Nationalmuseum, Weimar

It doesn't take much to make your own silhouette: a strong flashlight or other light source, some dark cardboard or poster board, a sharpened pen or pencil, and, of course, a pair of scissors.
Tape the cardboard to the wall. Then have the person you are portraying stand sideways in front of the wall and shine the light on the person. You'll have to experiment a little to find the right distance. Then draw along the outer edge of the shadow. When you're finished, cut out the silhouette and glue it onto a light-colored sheet of paper. You can make it look like a real picture by framing it.

Goethe in Profile, 1774,
Silhouette in Ink

So now that you know what Goethe looked like, try to tell which one of these silhouettes is a real portrait of him.

J.   W.   V.   G.

Find out on page 84.

Thrifty Portraits

The silhouette was also a popular form of portraiture in France for a while, and this is where the word comes from. It is named after a French finance minister, Étienne de Silhouette, who was very careful with money. Since a silhouette was relatively inexpensive to produce, it was the form of art Monsieur Silhouette liked best.

People even joked that instead of actual furniture, the finance minister had black 'profiles' hanging up all around his house. Everyone found this funny, and the cartoonists and artists had their hands full making different portraits of him in the form of these profiles. Thrifty portraits of a finance minister … how appropriate! Ever since then, such profile portraits have been called silhouettes.

Is Beauty Always the Same?

What does "beautiful" actually mean?

People around the world and through-out history have tried to answer these questions. And they've come up with very different answers. During times when there wasn't enough to eat, fat stomachs and double chins were often considered attractive. In ancient China, a beautiful woman was supposed to have very small feet. And today many people find body piercings beautiful, while others find them terrible.

Nefertiti, ca. 1360 BC,
Egyptian Museum, Berlin

What do you find beautiful in a face? Should it be well-proportioned and bright, finely formed with red lips and large eyes...?

Let's set the time machine to about 3,350 years ago and travel straight back to ancient Egypt, to the workshop of the sculptor Thutmosis. There, a bust of an intelligent and beautiful woman is being made. She is a queen, which you can see by her crown. It covers her head like a tall, blue helmet. **This queen's name is Nefertiti,** which means **"the beautiful one has come."** And it's still true today: her enchanting beauty still shines through.

Nefertiti's skin is taut and light brown, her lips are red. Her almond-shaped eyes are outlined in black and sparkle as if the sun god Re himself were present. Today this kind of eye makeup is called **"kohl."** It's hard to believe that some things - like makeup - were so similar even three thousand years ago.

Today people use kohl to emphasize the eyes and make them appear larger. Back then, **men and children** also used the black makeup around their eyes. It was believed that makeup swallowed the rays of the sun and protected the eyes from bright sunlight. Kohl was made by mixing soot, galena (lead sulfide), and other substances in small alabaster bowls. Then it was carefully applied with thin sticks. Even though Kohl contains lead, which can be poisonous, it is mixed in a way that can make the lead harmless. Kohl may even have protected ancient Egyptians from germs lurking around the swampy Nile river area.

Nefertiti can also give you other beauty tips from the past. It's easy to make a facial mask out of honey, for example.

Mix 2 tablespoons of honey into a paste and add a pinch of jelly-like agar agar. Let the mixture cool and then spread it over your face. You'll soon look just like Nefertiti. Well, almost....

GODDESSES OF LOVE

They look out at us from the pages
of newspapers and magazines:
models with self-confident smiles
and great bodies.

You might even ask yourself:
Are these people for real?
(Well ... no, they're not: these pictures
are heavily altered on the computer.)

But are only well-proportioned bodies
and perfect faces beautiful? Or do all
people have their own beauty, just as
nature made them? Many artists were
thinking about these questions 500
years ago, during the Renaissance,
and they came up with this answer:

**beauty requires both
elegant proportions and
natural grace.**

Sandro Botticelli, **The Birth of Venus**,
ca. 1493, Uffizi, Florence

Sandro Botticelli, a master Renaissance painter of Florence, Italy, painted the most beautiful woman ever: Venus, the goddess of love.

Do you think she's as beautiful as a goddess?

Well, she would certainly get a modeling contract. Her skin is as smooth and pale as alabaster. He long hair flies in the wind and glitters like gold in the fleeting rays of sun. She's definitely beautiful. She seems perfect, as if she's not from our own world. Maybe this is why she's not looking at us. No, this can't be a real woman, only an ideal. Such perfect beauty doesn't really exist. Or does it?

"Is that Simonetta?" whispered people who saw the painting at the time. Simonetta Vespucci was the wife of a Florentine merchant. She was revered as the "queen of beauty", and Botticelli painted her often. Florentine prince Giuliano de Medici is supposed to have been very much in love with her. And, as with many great romantic love stories, this one too was supposedly unhappy and ended in death. **Love is transient.** But Simonetta Vespucci's beauty endures for us through the paintings of Botticelli.

What would Venus look like today? Try this out yourself: It's well known that clothes make the person. On page 87 you'll find patterns for Venus's wardrobe that you can cut out. You can give her a modern look with sunglasses, a cap, and jewelry ...

Find out how on page 87.

One thing is clear: beauty can be captured in paintings and sculptures. You can see it. But can you also feel it? Of course! **Beauty is magical and radiates out into the world.** Sometimes it lights up a whole room.

Empress Theodora, 6th century, Mosaic in San Vitale, Ravenna

THE LOVELY THEODORA

As soon as you enter this little church in Ravenna, Italy, you're at a loss for words. Wow: so many tiny **mosaic stones** (tesserae) on the floor, the walls, and the ceiling! Thousands upon thousands of tesserae in every imaginable color look like they're trying to outshine one another. Some of them even contain silver or real gold leaf. They shine like stars in the firmament of a mysterious heavenly world. And there on the side wall, you can see an image of the powerful and beautiful **Byzantine empress Theodora.**

How is it possible to make such a picture with tesserae alone? In fact, it's not so easy. Empress Theodora is wearing a crown, strings of pearls, and a necklace of **oval emeralds** as signs of her dignity. These signs are how we can still recognize her even today, almost 1,500 years later. But her face, with its strong eyebrows and flat, straight nose are also depicted very precisely. From her mosaic portrait you can easily imagine that she was **a stern and powerful woman.**

Find out how on page 86.

Try laying a face with tesserae yourself.

Beauty radiates outwardly. This is clear from the Byzantine mosaics. But beauty also comes from inside. When you feel happy and confident, you automatically look much nicer. **So beauty is also a feeling.** That's why it's not possible to hold onto it or chase after it.

That's also why on many cat-walks in the modern world, beauty does not always look the same as it did in earlier times. For most models and fashion icons of today, beauty comes in very different porportions than it did for Botticelli and his fellow artists. Times change. Today, being thin is often in demand. **Everyone has to decide for themselves** what they find beautiful and what they need to feel comfortable about themselves.

Sometimes, however, it seems as if one of Botticelli's angels has just landed on the cat-walk in our day. What do you think of the hazy white silk dress that the woman on this cat-walk is wearing?

Cariactures and other Funny Portraits

Do you sometimes like to doodle and draw funny figures or strange faces? Relaxing, isn't it? Many famous artists have also tried out "finger warm-ups" like these, including Leonardo da Vinci. **Disfiguring heads in such a comical way is a special skill,** since no matter how funny they are, the people portrayed have to remain recognizable. What's most important is that the picture reveals the person's character. And not everyone depicted in a portrait has found their image so funny.

Leonardo da Vinci,
Five Grotesque Heads,
ca. 1487,
Windsor Castle,
Royal Library, London

Finding the Animal in You

The French caricaturist Grandville created his own unique world of portraits. **Hybrid figures** of people and animals were his great passion, which is also why he made so many drawings that combined **people with animal heads** or other animal features. Not only were these funny, but they allowed him to satirize specific human characteristics.

Claude Monet, **Man with a Straw Hat,** detail, ca. 1875, Musée Marmottan, Paris

Grandville also liked to transform human faces into animal faces. Only a few steps … and a man becomes a frog.

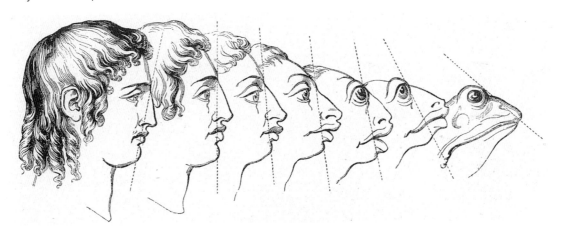

J. J. Grandville, **Comparison between Human and Animal Heads** 1844

Some sitters came off particularly badly. It's not often flattering to be compared to an **animal.** What do you think? Which human characteristics might these animals stand for?

Find out how on page 84.

Connect each animal figure with a characteristic.

cunning   snake   rabbit   fox   stubbornness   donkey   cowardice   deviousness

chez Aubert Passage Vero Dodat.

Est 490

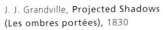

J. J. Grandville, **Projected Shadows**
(Les ombres portées), 1830

This is me in twenty years.

Here's some space for you to paint your future.

Guess the Occupation

Do you remember **the first thing you wanted to be when you grew up**: a doctor, a singer, a dancer, a pilot…? What would you have looked like? What would you have worn: a doctor's white coat, a pilot's glasses, maybe a ballerina's pointe shoes on your feet?

Sometimes it's not so easy to recognize someone's occupation at first glance. **Can you guess what the people on the following pages do for a living?**

Let's get started and travel into the past, to the year 1532. The German painter Hans Holbein the younger has painted the **portrait of an impressive gentleman** with rich clothing. He looks out at us proudly. He's probably very successful.

Find out more on page 84.

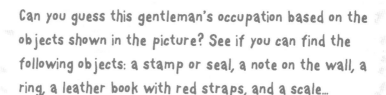

Can you guess this gentleman's occupation based on the objects shown in the picture? See if you can find the following objects: a stamp or seal, a note on the wall, a ring, a leather book with red straps, and a scale…

Hans Holbein the Younger, **Portrait of Geo Gisze**, 1532, Gemäldegalerie, Berlin State Museums, Berlin

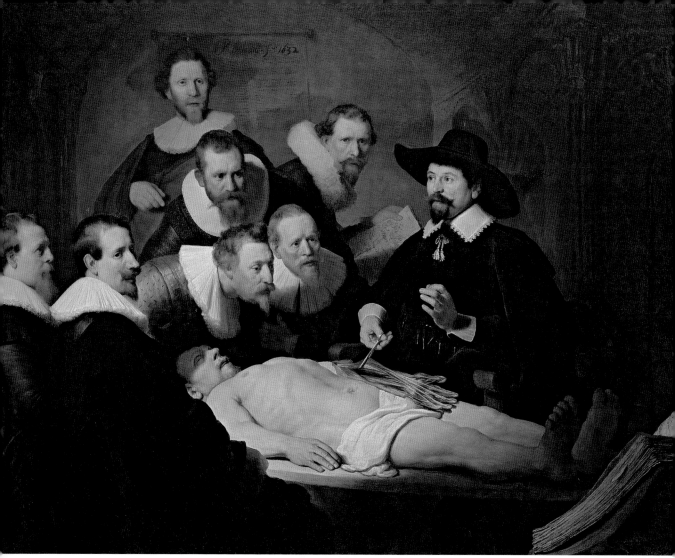

Rembrandt van Rijn, 1632,
Mauritshuis, The Hague

The Dutch painter Rembrandt van Rijn painted this eerie scene exactly a hundred years after
Holbein's painting. When several people are portrayed together in the same picture, like

 here, it is called a **group portrait.** Today this picture seems a bit like a scene from a
film, after someone had put the movie on pause! There are two leading actors
here: one is very much alive, while the other is as dead as a doornail.

The occupation of the man with the hat is immediately
clear. Notice the instrument in his hand.

Find out
more on
page 84.

Jan Vermeer,
1668,
Louvre, Paris

This gentleman wears a broad blue cloak and turns a **ball.** with his thumb. But what exactly is this picture showing?

Once you figure it out, you'll also know the occupation of this man, who was portrayed by the Dutch painter Jan Vermeer. Here's a clue: the map in the background shows the orbits of the planets.

Find out more on page 84.

One thing is clear right away: The imposing gentleman in this picture, who appears beneath a giant **red velvet baldachin,** is certainly **very important.** The symbols of his royal status have been placed beside him. **We look up at him from a lower vantage point.** His left arm is braced against his hip, and he turns self-confidently to face us. There's no need to think very long about which occupation is being shown here. But was that clothing really very comfortable? It must have been pretty hot beneath that **wig with its profuse curls.** And look at those shoes! How could he even walk in them?

Hyacinthe Rigaud, 1701 - 02, Louvre, Paris

Can you guess his occupation?

Find out on page 84.

What occupation is depicted in this portrait of a famous scholar?

Guiseppe Arcimboldo, ca. 1566, Skokloster Castle

Is this supposed to be a person? Or is it a **book-worm** composed only of books, with a curtain for his coat? Was the artist serious? There doesn't seem to be much resemblance to a real person here, wouldn't you agree? But when Italian artist Giuseppe Arcimboldo painted this portrait at the court of **Emperor Maximilian II** in Vienna, people recognized the sitter immediately.

Find out on page 84.

Do You Recognize Anyone?
Stars and Famous People

Now here's a colorful king! Frederick the Great, also called Old Fritz, was a German ruler during the 1700s. He reigned over a land called Prussia, which is now part of northern Germany. Painters often portrayed Frederick in his famous three-cornered hat. This picture, however, was made centuries after the king's death, and it shows Old Fritz **in very bright colors**. Yet the open-minded Frederick would surely have admired it. The portrait was created by Andy Warhol - who liked to poke fun at everyone - and he gave the Prussian ruler a completely **new look**. Even the three-cornered hat is missing!

Or we could follow the example of Wilhelm Busch - a caricaturist with a good sense of humor - and simply draw both hat and ruler ...

For starters - and this should be fun - our first mark must be a simple one.

Second, just on a lark, we'll extend it with another mark.

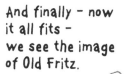

And third, not to be boorish, we'll add to it this flourish.

Fourth, and with the best of cheer, we'll construct this image here.

And finally - now it all fits - we see the image of Old Fritz.

How would you like to be famous? Would you be a singer or a president? How about a campaigner for human rights like Nelson Mandela?

Andy Warhol, **Frederick the Great,** 1986, Estate of Andy Warhol

Andy Warhol: "In the future everyone will be world-famous for fifteen minutes."

The Little Prince

Look out! The prince may just **leap right out of the picture!**
The Spanish prince Balthasar Charles cuts quite a dashing figure
on his pony. Not bad for a six-year-old. But as the **future monarch**
he didn't really have a choice. Riding lessons were a requirement
for members of the Spanish royal family, as was good behavior.
Spanish court painter Diego Velázquez depicted Balthasar Charles
here **with great dignity,** with his general's staff in his right hand.
The prince looks a lot less like a six-year-old boy than he does an
equestrian statue.

Have you always wanted to pose as a ruler? At the back
of this book you'll find the outline of the prince, which you
can color. You can also add a photo of your own face on the
outline. It's the quickest way to become a prince!

See
page 89.

Diego Velázqu
The Infant Pri
Balthasar Cha
Riding a Ho
ca. 1635, Mu
del Prado, Ma

Come on Up!

Can you hear what she's saying? This very famous lady is asking you to stop by and visit: "Why don't you come up sometime and see me …? Take a look around. **My mouth is a soft, pink sofa.** Make yourself comfortable. On my nose you'll find a very attractive **fireplace.** Read the time on the old clock: it's just before noon. I'm afraid my **blonde curls** aren't arranged today, dear. But you can see that they're nothing but a **curtain.**

Why don't you close them for me, honey? It's time for lunch."

"I've often wondered if this is really me. Is this actually my portrait? I've got a face that looks like you could walk around in it, **as if you were on stage,** and it doesn't seem to belong to me anymore. The artist Salvador Dalí wanted to construct me in his house in Figueres, Spain. But really, Salvador, a **room as a face!** My face as an actual room! I'm not so sure I like the idea, honey. But you can always come up sometime and see me."

Maybe you'd also like to represent someone in this way?

Find out on page 84.

And now for a real picture puzzle: The curtain rises. Is that a stage? Is it a screen? Do you recognize the face? Can you guess what this woman's occupation was?

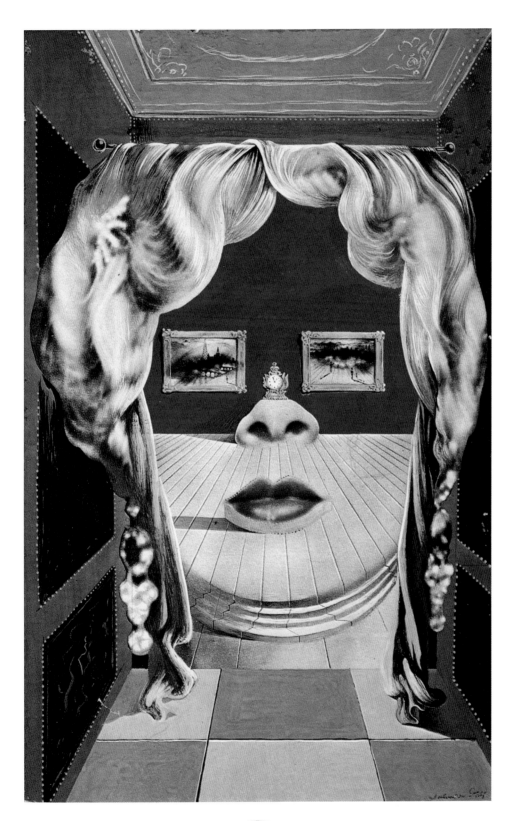

Salvador Dalí,
**Mae West's
Face, which
May be Used
as a Surrealist
Apartment,**
1934–35,
The Art Institute
of Chicago

Gustave Courbet, **The Desperate Man**, 1844–45, private collection

Artists Painting Themselves

When you look **in the mirror** in the morning, you can see right away whether you're starting your day out tired or bright-eyed and bushy-tailed. But the mirror says even more about you: how your eyes, nose, and mouth look and whether your face is more round or more oval-shaped. It also shows you how everything changes, everyday.

This is why using your mirror image to make a portrait is always **a bit of an adventure**. But with the tips explained here, you'll soon get it right.

How to draw your self-portrait:
First look carefully at your face: Is it round, oval-shaped, square, or long and thin?

Your eyes are about halfway between the top and bottom of your face. What shape are they, large and round or almond-shaped? The colored part of the eye, the iris, is usually brown, blue, or green. What eye color do you have? The small black dot in the center of the eye is the pupil. How far apart are your eyes? In many faces, the distance between them is about the width of an eye.

What shape are your eyebrows? Do they curve upwards or fall steeply down-wards? Are they thick or more delicate? The eyebrows frame your eyes and help to determine your facial expression.
Look at your nose. Is it wide or thin? Begin with the sides of the nose and the nostrils. Shadows to the left and right show that the nose sticks out from the face.

Now comes the mouth. Follow the outer corner of your mouth upwards to your eyes. This way you can measure how wide to draw your lips.

Are you finished drawing your face? Check again in the mirror.
Does it look like you?

Albrecht Dürer, **Self-Portrait**, 1500, Alte Pinakothek, Munich

Role Playing

A self-portrait has always been **a great challenge** for any artist. Many artists **slipped into a role** when they portrayed themselves or experimented with their mirror image.

This artist has used great precision in depicting his curling hair, his face, and the fine fur he's wearing. His facial features have also been painted with just as much devotion and **fidelity.** The artist's dog apparently thought so too, because supposedly he tried to lick his master's self-portrait. At least that's what people said at the time …

The painter was Albrecht Dürer. He was twenty-eight when he painted this self-portrait, from which he looks directly out at you.
And yet there's something strange about his posture and his gaze …

Find out on page 84.

If you suspect that the artist has slipped into a kind of role, you're right. Can you figure out which one? Does this picture remind you of anything?

Henri Rousseau called the picture to the right "Myself." **Pretty self-confident!**

The former tax official stands proudly with his palette and brush before a bridge, symbolizing his new occupation. He's grown large and is filled with pride. He's finally taken on the role of an admired painter.

Henri Rousseau, **Myself, Portrait-Landscape**, 1890, Nationalgalerie, Prague

Rousseau painted himself in the city of art, the place of his desires. And just to make sure that everyone knew where this place was supposed to be, Rousseau included an **important identifying symbol** of the city in the background.

Do you recognize the symbol and do you know where the artist painted this self-portrait?

Find out on page 84.

Parmigianino,
**Self-Portrait
in a Convex
Mirror,** 1523 - 24,
Kunsthistorisches
Museum, Vienna

Simply "Look around the Corner"

How old would you guess the man in the picture is? He's just barely twenty-one years old.

And he was not yet very well known when he gave Pope Clement VII this self-portrait as

a special gift. It was so unusual that the pope surely took note of the young artist.

The idea occurred to him one morning as he was shaving. Back then people used so-called **barber's mirrors.** These mirrors were **convex,** or curved outward, and they **enlarged** the image. Today, barbers' mirrors are sometimes used as traffic mirrors to help drivers in places where visibility is poor. Department stores also use them to detect people trying to steal merchandise. Such mirrors make it possible to "see around the corner," so to speak: **very useful for self-portraits.**

The Italian painter Parmigianino also thought so. He placed his right hand with the drawing chalk directly in front of the mirror. This is why it appears so exaggeratedly large. The room behind the painter seems to be curved like a ball. To make it seem especially "real," Parmigianino painted his portrait on a curved piece of wood: a brilliant idea, executed with the skill of a master. The pope was delighted.

Try it yourself. If you don't have a convex mirror handy, then a soup spoon will also do.
Look at yourself in the convex surface and you'll see how your face is distorted, like in Parmigianino's self-portrait. It makes sense that the artist drew so much attention to his hand; that's what he draws with, after all. What's the most important part of your self-portrait?

Vincent Van Gogh,
**Self-Portrait
with Bandaged
Ear**, 1889,
Courtauld Gallery,
London

The Sad Artist

Here another artist has painted himself. **Do you think he looks happy?** He used flickering yellow and green paint to capture his thin, angular face. Is he ill? His eyes look sad and tired. Vincent van Gogh is the name of this artist, and he lived a tumultuous life. But Vincent had a special gift. He was able to show his own inner **turmoil** on a canvas, using intense **colors and agitated brushstrokes.** What is that wrapped around his head? It looks like a white bandage. Do you know Vincent's story?

The Fight

The sun and warmth drew the artist from the cold northern climate of Holland to the southern French town of Arles. For a brief period he lived there together with fellow artist Paul Gauguin. Apparently the two had a terrible fight, and in a fit of **rage and despair** van Gogh seriously injured his own ear. Even today one can still feel the **pain, grief, and loneliness** in his self-portrait.

Another picture can also be seen in van Gogh's self-portrait, right next to his head. This picture is a **Japanese woodcut.** Such prints were **very popular in Europe** at the time, and many artists enthusiastically collected them. You can try out the technique yourself!

You'll need a linoleum sheet, a v-shaped chisel or gouge, a piece of hard plastic, a roller and ink, and heavy paper for printing. But be sure to get permission from your parents before you start.

First, cover your working space with newspaper. Then transfer your drawing to the linoleum sheet. Use your chisel or gouge to cut away everything that you want to be white in the finished picture. Only the lines and areas that you want to print in color should remain uncut.

Then squeeze some ink onto the plastic and roll over it several times with the roller. Now use the roller to transfer the ink onto your linocut. Be careful: the cutout parts of the linoleum sheet have to remain free of ink. Firmly press the inked side of the linocut onto the paper, carefully remove it, and let the print dry.

Mary Cassatt,
Little Girl in a
Blue Armchair,
1878, National
Gallery of Art,
Washington D.C.

Children, Children, Paint Me Please!

Who is the little girl loafing around in the blue armchair in Mary Cassatt's picture? She's sprawled out nonchalantly, her arm behind her head and her legs dangling. Her eyes seem about to fall shut. She's so tired … and **so completely relaxed**.

The dog has curled up **snugly** on the armchair to the left. He's just as tired as his friend. Do you also have a pet?

The little girl here is "dog tired." What might a picture look like that shows someone as clever as a fox? Or a strong as a bear? What other comparisons can you think of?

Édouard Manet portrayed his godson Léon in this picture (to the right) over 150 years ago. Can you tell what he's doing? That's right, he's blowing **soap bubbles**.

You can make your own soap bubbles by mixing dishwashing soap and water together. To make really good bubbles, try adding a bit a glycerin. But be sure to get your parents' permission.

Édouard Manet,
Soap Bubbles,
1867,
Gulbenkian
Collection,
Lisbon

Pablo Picasso,
Girl with a Boat
(Maya Picasso),
1938, Museum
Collection
Rosengart,
Lucerne

It's Maya!

What is she looking at? **Is that even a face?** Yes, you can definitely make out a girl. Her eyes are **askew,** but you can find them right away. The nose is a bit more difficult to detect. And her mouth is right where it should be, on a **yellow triangle!** Her legs are covered by white pants, and her hands are holding onto a **sailboat**.

This is Maya, the daughter of the famous painter Pablo Picasso. Did he really paint like this? Here you can see Maya from the front and the side at the same time, as if he had broken her down **into individual shapes** and then reassembled them.

Picasso played with colors and forms like a little child would. Maybe this is why he always said, **"It took me a lifetime to paint like a child."** This would mean that you too are just the right age to become an artist. So what are you waiting for?

You are Picasso!
To make a collage you'll need photographs of yourself or your family or friends, heavy construction paper, glue, and scissors. Cut the photographs apart and reassemble the separate pieces onto the construction paper. Maybe you'd like to try giving yourself two noses or four arms. Or you could become a four-headed snake and draw a body for yourself. You can also cut your photos into geometric shapes and piece them together like a puzzle. There are no limits to your imagination ...
Will you recognize yourself when you're finished?

Mäda the Flower Girl

Here you see flowers everywhere you look: on her dress, in her hair. Flowers are raining onto a floor of flowers. Mäda Primavesi is standing in the middle of spring. Could this be a play on her name, which sounds like "primavera," the Italian word for "spring"? Mäda is nine. Her father, Otto Primavesi, was the banker and financier of the Wiener Werkstätten, a famous artist's workshop founded in Vienna. Gustav Klimt was a member of the workshop, and he painted this portrait for Mäda's father. **"Look at me!" Mäda seems to be saying,** as if we could do anything else! Her gaze is so open and intent, it's almost as if she's speaking directly to us. **It would sure be fun to know her.**

How does Mäda seem to you?

diligent

helpful   defiant

friendly

fun   quiet/calm

petulant

serious   shy

impertinent

wild

Friends painting each other:
How about making a portrait of one of your friends? Sit across from each other and look into each other's eyes. What color are they? And what shapes are your faces? What kind of an expression can you see in them?
Your mouths and eyebrows offer the first clues. What kinds of clothing are you wearing? Maybe you'd like to depict each other in old-fashioned outfits from another century, or with your favorite game or animal.
Go for it. In a picture, anything goes!

Gustav Klimt,
**Portrait
of Mäda
Primavesi,**
ca. 1912,
Metropolitan
Museum of
Art, New York,

Masks: Make Yourself Invisible

Masks give you a chance to hide and become someone completely different, maybe someone bold and outspoken or someone a bit crazy. A mask conceals you and protects you. Masks have always done this, in every culture throughout the world.

Not only did masks offer protection from evil forces and diseases, they also played a central role in many festivals. Masks radiate their own magic, even those in paintings. Artists have often borrowed the power and energy of masks, their striking colors and forms, and created something very special with them.

Have you noticed that when you put on a mask, you can take on its character and expression. Many of the masks in Emil Nolde's picture (to the left) seem pretty eerie, like the old man with the poison-green face and the snow-white beard. Do you know how to mix this shade of green? It used to be made from the chemicals verdigris and arsenic, both of which are poisonous. That's why we still sometimes hear the expression "poison green." But there's no need to worry anymore: Today we have artificial colors. Which ones would you mix to get such a "poisonous" shade?

The Poison – Green Face

Life is wild and colorful. And so are the images of the Expressionists. These painters were able to express their feelings with glowing colors and unusual forms.

For them, painting things just as they looked was much too dull. That's why their horses are sometimes blue, their cows yellow, and their faces sometimes colorful masks. The German artist Emil Nolde loved masks. Together with his wife, he went travelling in the South Seas. He was so delighted by what he saw that he later began painting pictures of masks instead of portraits.

Find out on page 84.

You can construct a mask like this yourself. Draw it on a sheet of heavy paper or cardboard and cut around the edges. Then you can paint it with the "poison green" you mixed yourself. You can use cotton balls to add a white beard.

Mask Magic

Various masked dancers of the Bwa people waiting to perform on a market day in Boni, Burkina Faso, 1985

Hyenas have always been considered viscious and dangerous. The mouth of this long-eared hyena mask is thus decorated with two rows of teeth. African masks were worn during **special ritual acts** by tribal chiefs, and they were used as a way of communicating with gods or spirits. Only those who closely observed the movements of the masked dancers would be able to understand their magic. A **strange and mysterious world** would open up. But maybe you too can discover these secrets if you make and wear a similar mask …

It's easiest to make masks when there are two of you. You'll need **plaster bandages** (from the pharmacy or crafts store), some string, a bowl of **water**, and **Vaseline** or another oil-based cream. First, cover your face with a thick layer of the cream, being careful not to forget the eyebrows and the hairline. Then cut the plaster bandages into short strips and place them in the water. Once they are soft, you can lie down and have your friend place some of them over your face in several layers. It's best to have a parent or other adult help with this process, to be sure that your nostrils are left free and you can breathe easily. Remove the finished mask from your face as soon as it's firm. Then you can place the remaining plaster bandages on your friend's face, again making sure to keep the nostrils free. Finally, once both masks have been removed and are completely dry, decorate them any way you'd like. You can then poke two small holes in the sides, just about where your ears are, and thread a cord through them. Tie this cord behind your head when you wear the mask.

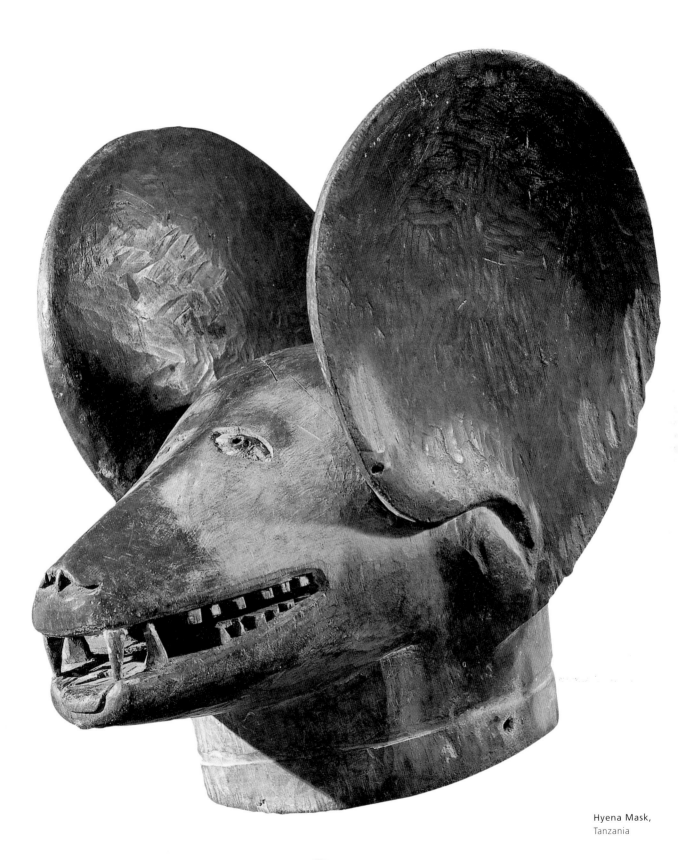

Hyena Mask,
Tanzania

You and Me Together

A **double portrait** shows two people in the same
picture. To take a second look …

An old man and a young boy can be seen in this picture: maybe **a grandfather and
his grandson?** The old man wears a dark red mantle with fur trim, the boy a red
cape and cap. **Red is warm; it's the color of love**. Love doesn't care whether someone is beautiful, young, or old. It also doesn't care if someone has a diseased and
disfigured nose, like the grandfather in this picture. The way these two look into each
other's eyes shows great **trust** and **affection,** which can be felt throughout the
whole picture. The Florentine painter Ghirlandaio wanted to show the power of love
to overcome all external things.

Red is the color of love. Red is also the color of
this love punch.
To make it you'll need:
1 package of frozen mixed berries
1 package of frozen raspberries or strawberries
1 quart red fruit juice (red currant, grape, or
cranberry juice)
1 bottle of sparkling water
Strawberry or raspberry syrup

Let the fruit thaw out and chop it into small
pieces. Then pour the juices over it and add
syrup. The red love punch is finished!

Domen
Ghirlanda
Old Man wi
a Young B
after 14
Louvre, Pa

Grant Wood,
**American
Gothic,** 1930,
Friends of
American
Art Collection,
The Art Institute
of Chicago
and VAGA,
New York

A Famous Couple

Would you agree that the man in this painting, who is peering through his round glasses, looks very **stern?** The **pitchfork** in his hand doesn't exactly look inviting. Is this any way to greet visitors? The woman beside him seems **old-fashioned,** with her little white collar and her brooch. Is this **a husband and wife** in front of their house?

The painter Grant Wood happened to see this house one day as he was driving by. He must have liked how it looked, especially its pointed attic window. While travelling through the American Midwest, he **observed the people who lived out in the country and painted them.**

But the Midwesterners didn't particularly like this picture. Was he trying **to mock** them? They didn't see themselves as so suspicious and hostile-looking. Is the picture a joke, or is it meant to be taken seriously? What do you think Grant Wood wanted to say with it? Even today, the experts are not really sure.

Incidentally, the painter used his sister Nan and his dentist as models for the woman and man in his picture. They "played the roles" of the famers, so to speak. So the picture didn't come about completely by accident, after all.

In fact, many people have used this picture to poke fun at themselves or others. In the back of the book you will find Grant Wood's couple once again. Try making them look as strange and unfamiliar as possible. For example, you might draw a microphone or a funny hat where the pitchfork is supposed to be.
Use your imagination.
Maybe the picture inspires you to play the role of a farmer yourself?
You and a friend could dress up like Grant Wood's characters -- or take on whatever roles you like best!

Find out how on page 86

Love as Light as a Feather

Have you ever been **in love?** Suddenly you have **butterflies** in your stomach, and maybe you feel as if **you could fly away** like them. This is what it must have been like for the painter Marc Chagall when he married his wife Bella. Their marriage took place the very same year he painted this picture. It was a warm summer in 1915. **Like a bride,** Bella holds a **colorful bouquet of summer flowers** in her hand. She **floats** happily with her husband through the picture. In real life, whenever Bella visited her husband's studio, she always brought along the nicest things: a cake (which you can see on the table) and other good things to eat, fresh flowers, love, and of course, herself. **For the painter, every day with Bella was like a birthday.**

What do you do when you want to **remember someone forever?** Maybe you draw or paint the people you love together in a picture. Or maybe you take their photo and hang it up in a frame so you can look at it anytime you want.

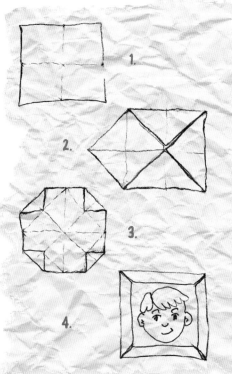

1.

2.

3.

4.

It's easy to make a picture frame:
You'll need **construction paper or heavy metal foil** and a **hook** (from an office supply store).

Cut out a square from the construction paper and fold it over twice in the center so that the folds form a cross. Open it and smooth it out. Then take the four corners and fold each one toward the center. Now open it all up again and fold the four corners down a final time to the folds nearest them. You can then place your picture or photo in the frame and fold over the edges. Finally, all that's left to do is glue the frame down.

Marc Chagall, **Birthday**, 1915,
Museum of Modern Art, New York

Frida Kahlo,
**Self-Portrait
with Thorn
Necklace**, 1940,
Harry Ransom
Center,
The University of
Texas at Austin

Can the Soul Be Painted?

Can you paint what you feel? And feel what you paint? It's not really so easy to say. Feelings are **confusing** and sometimes seem **like a roller coaster ride:** up and down, sad or happy.

But it's also possible **to see** feelings, not only on your face but also in your whole posture. In art, feelings can become visible. They take the form of **colors and shapes,** and they can be **lively, anxious, or calm.** Sometimes they become symbols or signs that hint at or point to something else. Try this yourself sometime and see how the pictures in your head appear on paper. Your picture should show what you feel, like **a reflection of your soul.**

Evil Spirits Be Gone!

Frida, the woman in the picture to the right, has magical powers. The black cat slinks on velvet paws along with her. Memories can be like a cage. But if you put them in a picture, you might be able to find a way out. **Symbols** can help you do this; they can act like magical powers. Frida is wearing a thorn necklace that pricks her neck. This is how she painted her pain, which she suffered as the result of an illness and a terrible accident. A pendant in the form of a bird dangles from the necklace. Like the monkey on her shoulder, it is meant to protect her from lovesickness. Frida's flowers can fly, and the wall of leaves protects the artist from anything that might hurt her. In this way the symbols take on a **healing power.**

A talisman acts in a similar way. You only have to believe in it. If you like, you can make your own … something that looks like your favorite animal or your own sign or symbol. You can use soapstone, which carves easily. You'll also need some files and some sandpaper to carve the finer details. You could even try to recreate the bird from Frida's thorn necklace.

Dancing Colors

Is that a man or a woman? The red clothing flickers restlessly against the light-colored background with its shades of turquoise, blue, and green. The painter, Russian artist Alexej Jawlensky, has surrounded his figure with a thick black outline. The eyes, lined in black, look out intensely from beneath the dark hair. A rose appears in the buttonhole, and a mysterious smile is seen on the face. Jawlensky has painted the dancer Alexander Sacharoff, who is already made up for his performance. Just as his dance will use movement to express sensations and feelings, the painter has created his own mood with colors.

Make your own colorful face: Use a black crayon to draw a head, eyes, nose, and mouth. Then use watercolors to "fill in" the face. You can either paint separate areas of color next to each other or use water to let the colors flow and mix together. For the background, choose a color that fits the mood of the face. Do you feel like using soft pink tones to make the face look cheerful and bright? Or would you rather have a dark-colored background to give your figure a scarier or more intense look? You'll soon see how a different expression is created each time.

Alexej Jawlensky, **Portrait of the Dancer Alexander Sacharoff**, 1909,
Städtische Galerie im Lenbachhaus, Munich

Colorful Screen Dots

Roy Lichtenstein, **M-Maybe. (A Girl's Picture)**, 1965, Museum Ludwig, Cologne

Roy Lichtenstein always had a soft spot for **comics**. At some point he hit upon the idea of enlarging individual pictures onto his canvas with a projector. In this way, he could reproduce the images, change them, and make them his own.

Look carefully at a colored image in a newspaper or magazine. Take a magnifying glass and look even more closely. What do you see? Images like these are made up of countless tiny red, blue, yellow, and black dots. The same dots appear in Lichtenstein's pictures, only much bigger. These **small Ben-Day dots** made his pictures seem like printed reproductions from comic strips, and they became became his trademark.

So now we see the large picture by Lichtenstein, but we don't know what happens next to the girl. She seems to be worried. "Maybe he became ill and couldn't leave the studio," we read in the speech balloon. Can you finish the story?

How to paint a portrait like Lichtenstein: Look in a newspaper or comic book to find a story you like and trace the outlines onto a sheet of paper. Draw a border around it and then paint the different areas in different colors. Next, fill some of the areas with tiny, regularly-spaced colored dots like Lichtenstein did. You can make these dots easily by hand, or you can try using cotton swabs.

You can also cut out faces and other pictures from newspapers or magazines and combine them into comic strips. Be sure to make up your own speech balloons!

That Looks Just Like a Photo!

When you paint a portrait, you probably want it to look **as "real" as possible.** Everyone should be able to tell who the sitter is. And if your painting doesn't work out so well, you might find yourself reaching for the camera. But is it always so important to represent things **naturalistically?** Maybe a portrait can reveal something that isn't always seen in real life, or something that's never really been noticed before? **Painting gives you the freedom to play** with forms and colors so that something new is created. Photography can also do this, by the way, but it does so differently.

Eye Contact

What happens when you look at the picture from very close up and then when you move a bit further away?

Find out more on page 84.

Is this a photograph? Maybe a passport photo. **Could it be a painting?** It could and it is. It was created by American artist Chuck Close, who can make paintings that look like photos. And it's no wonder, since he used a photograph as a model. He reproduces everything **very exactly,** down to the smallest pore. In the end you stand before the picture astonished. The image has become so large that it's almost as if you were looking at a screen in a movie theater, only at a picture that doesn't move. But the artist does seem to speak to you through the look in the woman's eyes: "I wanted to paint a giant picture that blows you away." And it does.

Chuck Close uses a special trick to transfer the photograph very exactly onto the canvas. Try using this method to paint yourself or a friend:
Take a photograph and, using a ruler and pen, cover it with evenly spaced horizontal and vertical lines. This will produce a grid of small squares, like that on graph paper. Next you must create a grid of similar, but larger, squares on a piece of paper. Now take a close look at each of the squares in the photograph and try to paint or draw them-square by square-as exactly as possible on the sheet of paper. This activity requires deep concentration and a lot of effort. But it works!

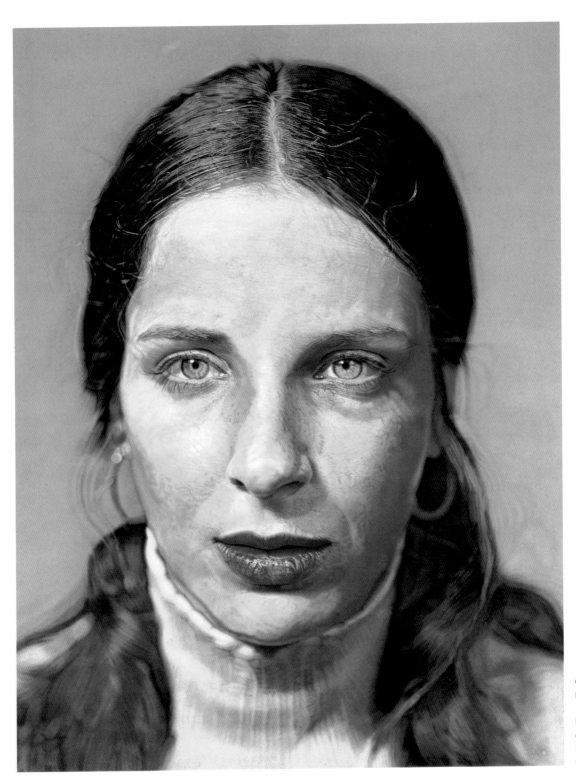

Chuck Close,
Leslie,
1972-73,
Private
collection,
Rutherford,
California

Gerhard Richter,
Betty, 1988,
The Saint Louis
Art Museum,
Saint Louis

The Girl Who Simply Looks Away

Why is she looking away? There's no one behind her, only darkness. Too bad … you probably would have liked to see **her face.** But she doesn't seem to want to show it. So why on earth does she let herself be painted? **Can this even be considered a portrait?** Her jacket is beautiful; it looks soft and cozy. But everything's a bit **blurry.** Is this picture a photograph? Or is the photograph a picture? And who does it represent? Very confusing …

This is a portrait by German artist Gerhard Richter of his daughter Betty. Richter has made many portraits: some with paint and others with the camera. Sometimes it's hard to say from a distance whether a work of his is a painting or a photograph. What do you think this picture is, a **photograph or a painting?** – If you guessed that the turned-around Betty is a painting, you're right! Gerhard Richter often painted his pictures a bit blurry, like an out-of-focus photograph.

In the early years of photography, people believed photographs were superior to painting, because technology seemed to reproduce reality more closely than the hand of a painter. But anyone who is familiar with the greatest artists knows that this isn't true. Painting can do everything photography can do, and sometimes even more. For it can often show something about a person that is invisible to a camera.

Harsh!

Crime scene: Vienna's Westbahnhof train station at dusk. An inconspicuous man stands beside a **photo booth,** waiting impatiently for his photos to be ready. The same thing is repeated the next day, and the next day, and so on. Sometimes the man makes **funny grimaces.** Other times he strikes a **serious** pose. He can even have the photo booth spit out postcards with photos of his face on them. But for this man, the real work begins only after he gets his photos home. There **he enlarges the pictures and works them over,** often covering them with paint. To the right, you can see one of the results. The man now seems to be growing horns, and there's a spot of paint on his nose. Talk about **devilish!** He's winking at you: wink back!

(The "man," by the way, is the Austrian painter Arnulf Rainer.)

Now it's your turn. Take a photo of yourself, maybe with a grimace on your face, and print it out at a large size. Then get your paint, gather your ideas, and go for it! Feel free to poke a bit of fun at yourself as you make your artwork. Just don't be squeamish; Arnulf Rainer sure wasn't …

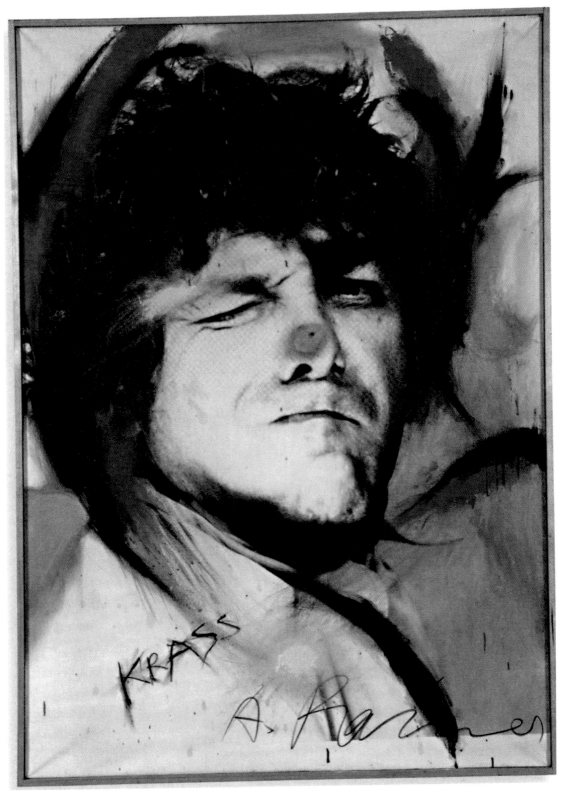

Arnulf Rainer,
Krass (Harsh),
1971/73,
possession of
the artist

Solutions

p. 20

V is right.

p. 31

fox cunning, snake deviousness, rabbit cowardice, donkey stubbornness

p. 34 - 35

The impressive gentleman is a **merchant (see the picture to the right)**.

p. 36

The "main character" is a **surgeon**.

The picture shows the surgeon Dr. Tulp (the highest ranking figure, with the hat). The dead man is Adriaan Adriaanszon, a highway robber who was hanged for his crimes. The doctor is explaining the skeletal muscles to his colleagues. To the lower right is an anatomy textbook. Observers of the anatomy lesson were required to pay admission.

p. 37

The man portrayed is an **astronomer**. The sphere is a celestial globe that shows the stars.

p. 38

The crown shown near the person to the left immediately betrays his "occupation": he is a king, of course. To be precise, this is a portrait of Louis XIV, former king of France.

p. 39

This gentleman is the **librarian** Wolfgang Lazius, a collector of rare books.

Martin Schongauer, **Christ Blessing**, ca. 1470, Uffizi, Florence

p. 44 - 45

Mae West was a well-known **actress** who can be seen in American films, especially those from the 1930s.

p. 48

The image is meant to resemble paintings of Jesus Christ, like the one shown here by Martin Schongauer. Dürer did this not only to depict himself as a pious Christian, but also to call attention to his role as a creative artist. What self-confidence!

p. 49

In the background of his picture, Rousseau painted the Eiffel Tower, which had just been finished the previous year for the city's world's fair. The Eiffel Tower is in **Paris**.

p. 63

yellow + blue = green. The more yellow you mix in, the lighter the green will become. A touch of white will make the green a bit softer.

p. 78 - 79

If you go very close to the picture, you'll see nothing but small dots of paint. If you move away from it, the countless dots of color will form the face of Leslie. This is because the eye perceives the colors as a picture only from a distance.

Rousseau, Detail Eiffel Tower

Arts and Crafts Ideas

p. 11

Make yourself a pair of cool glasses!

Copy or trace this pattern (you may need to make it somewhat larger), transfer it onto heavy paper or cardboard, and color it in. Then cut all the peices out, fold over the flaps on the temples, and glue the flaps onto the frame.

p. 13 Mona Lisa

Does this drawing remind you of a portrait that you've already seen in the book? That's right: it's Leonardo da Vinci's Mona Lisa. Here you can color her in.

p. 28 To make a mosaic you'll need:

tesserae (mosaic pieces), glue, a bag of plaster, a spatula or putty knife, and a sponge. Draw a face on a firm surface, such as a wooden board, a platter, or a can. Then glue on the tesserae. The face should be formed with pink stones. For the eyes, nose, mouth, and eyebrows you'll need dark red or brown stones, and for the highlights white ones are best. When you're done, mix the plaster with water and spread the mixture over the stones so that all the gaps between them are filled. Remove the excess plaster with a sponge and let the mosaic dry.

p. 68 – 69

This picture has often been used to poke fun at other people or at oneself. Here you have a chance to remake it:
What could the man be holding besides a pitchfork?

P. 27

Color the pieces of clothing with nice designs
and cut them out: new clothes for Venus!

p. 42 - 43

Glue your passport photo onto the space beneath the hat. You can design your prince's clothing to look just like the painting. Or, if you wish, put yourself in your own favorite clothes.

The Deutsche Nationalbibliothek lists this publication in the Deutsche Nationalbibliografie; detailed bibliographic information is available at http://dnb.d-nb.de.

Front cover: Amedeo Modigliani, Girl with Pigtails, 1918 (photograph: Artothek)
Frontispiece: Pinturicchio, Portrait of a young man, c. 1480/85 (photograph: Artothek)
Endpapers: Thomas Gainsborough, Mr. and Mrs. Andrews, c.1750 (photograph: Artothek)
Claude Monet, La Japonaise (Camille Monet in Japanese Costume), 1876 (photograph: Artothek)

Photo credits: If not otherwise stated, the original reproductions are from the archive of the publishing house. Philip Pikart p. 22; Getty p. 29; Artothek pp. 34, 35, 36, 43, 48, 57, 74, 84; (photograph: Peter Willi) p. 37; (Christie's Images Ltd) p. 3; akg-images p. 60

Prestel Verlag, Munich

Verlagsgruppe Random House GmbH
www.prestel.de

Translation: Cynthia Hall
Editing: Brad Finger
Design: Michael Schmölzl, agenten.und.freunde OHG, Munich
Production: Nele Krüger
Art direction: Cilly Klotz
Lithography: Reproline Mediateam, Munich
Printing and binding: Neografia, St. Martin

Verlagsgruppe Random House FSC-DEU-0100
The FSC-certified paper Hello Fat Matt 1,1 has been supplied by Condat, Le Lardin Saint-Lazare, France.

ISBN 978-3-7913-7100-9